ABIDE

*Crab Orchard Series in Poetry*

# ABIDE \ JAKE ADAM YORK

Crab Orchard Review
& Southern Illinois University Press
Carbondale

17  16  15  14    4  3  2  1

The Crab Orchard Series in Poetry is a joint publishing venture of Southern Illinois University Press and *Crab Orchard Review*. This series has been made possible by the generous support of the Office of the President of Southern Illinois University and the Office of the Vice Chancellor for Academic Affairs and Provost at Southern Illinois University Carbondale.

**Editor of the Crab Orchard Series in Poetry: Jon Tribble**

          Library of Congress Cataloging-in-Publication Data
York, Jake Adam.
[Poems. Selections]
Abide / Jake Adam York.
    pages   cm. — (Crab Orchard Series in Poetry)
ISBN 978-0-8093-3327-1 (paperback : alk. paper) — ISBN 0-8093-3327-9 (paperback : alk. paper) — ISBN 978-0-8093-3328-8 (ebook) — ISBN 0-8093-3328-7 (ebook)
I. Title.
PS3625.O747A6 2014
811'.6—dc23                                              2013032572

Printed on recycled paper. ♻

The paper used in this publication meets the minimum requirements of American National Standard for Information Sciences—Permanence of Paper for Printed Library Materials, ANSI Z39.48-1992. ∞

*for Sarah*

I am here because I could never get the hang of Time.
— Terrance Hayes

We are living in the moment when an indivisible world harmony and the conceptions it suggests are breaking up, a time when partial harmonies arise everywhere and converge toward a generalized disharmony, something the writer feels strongly he cannot explore without first renouncing this indivisibility that established him, sovereign and seer, in his place and words. To renounce the indivisible is to learn a new way of approaching the world; in doing so the writer learns to deploy all of his works in this approach, to become accustomed to this new and generalized disharmony while trying to follow its innumerable traces.
— Édouard Glissant

We work on the other side of time.
— Sun Ra

# CONTENTS

ABIDE

# Abide with Me

Fast falls the light.
Through the trees, the windows.
Through valances and dust.
Its fingers thin.
Its fingers flatten
and blush. One hand
on the cover, one
on my breath, you
ease me to the hour
when the clock forgets
its hands, a dream
of a lake I'd swim
years before we met
and the boathouse where I'd lie
inches from the water,
drying in afternoon.
You shake the light
from your shoulders,
it falls to the floor,
to the water where I swam
when the lake was my clock,
my dream, no hour,
no hands but yours,
if they dream us here.
The stereo takes back our breath.
All sound is light.
Your fingers pulling back
the dust, the curtains.
Pull back the curtains,
pull back the day
so we can fall
breathless into night.

## *te lyra pulsa manu* or
## something like that


As Ovid or Onomacritus—or was it Ike Turner?—said
     music makes everything want to reach out of itself,
rocks forgetting their gravity, birds hovering
     as if become part of the air itself,
and so the pines and the olives leaning over Orpheus
     as he slid the bottle along the guitar's neck
gave up their sap and oil which is why he glistened
     in the sun or the starlight and seemed to express
that brilliance, like a zoetrope or a planetarium,
     and you couldn't tell if he was gathering
or giving it back, but that's music,
     erupting beautiful and returning to itself at last,
Mercury's gift—the turtle's gut
     strung across its desiccated shell,
a melody pulled from such concentrated silence
     and returned to its bowl, making every ear
the parenthesis that separates us from persistence.
     But we want to last, at least long enough
to grasp what we've just let go, so
     the women, washing their clothes by the river,
hearing that song—its melody remembering
     then forgetting every one they knew—
left their clothes to froth on the river's shoals,
     to follow and catch and at last
to reach inside him for what they'd lost,
     pulling everything out,
which is how music entered the human world,
     a stain beneath the fingernails that tells
where you've been. His head, his guitar
     floated down the Hebrus to the sea
where Apollo raised the strings into the night
     making the turtle and the song immortal.

That, anyway, is how it was put to me
        in a juke-joint in Mississippi, as if
from Onomacritus to Ovid to Ike Zimmerman,
        who taught Robert Johnson how to play,
and when someone poisoned—or was it stabbed?—
        Johnson, for something he said,
like *Won't you squeeze my lemon*
        *till the juice runs down my leg*
or *I got a phonograph* . . . back, like a breath,
        into the world, the water, the earth,
the light. There is always someone there,
        Ovid should have said, to tear you apart
when you get beautiful enough, first just picking
        at the skin, the fingernail or tortoise-shell
plectrum a kind of tease, but then more strident,
        your corona zipped off and flattened to a disc.
This is how, in these moments, when music
        coaxes everything out of itself,
when you become so attuned
        you almost *hear* the light,
the pulse of the fluorescent tube
        over the bar or the cigarette machine
or the star, 900 years away,
        which is really two stars, eclipsing
then amplifying one another, this
        is how I imagine William Moore,
after walking from Chattanooga to Gadsden,
        with the sign, *Jesus Was an Alien*,
taped to his caisson, his letter for Ross Barnett—
        *Be gracious and give more*
*than is immediately demanded of you*—
        still folded in its envelope
when the assassin found him,
        and this is how I imagine
Medgar Evers, not two months later,
        the pulse of the kitchen light

reaching through the bullet hole in the window
          to flicker on his skin,
the one struck down on the night
          of the year's first Lyrids, the meteors
that seem to fall from the guitar in the sky
          like change passersby have thrown
through the sound hole, the other
          as the coins rang again on the dome of night,
and Zimmerman in the graveyard
          where he taught Johnson how to listen,
looking up through the trees and playing
          until the dew had fallen on him again
and he felt a music in his fingers
          he hadn't known for years. . . .
Maybe this is not what he meant,
          Ovid or Onomacritus or Ike
or whatever his name was
          when he told me the story
of the original bluesman
          that night at the bar in Mississippi,
but this is how I remember it
          when I see him, turning slowly
in the neon, as he reaches through the crowd,
          everyone reaching, gathering
beneath the fingernails, this is what I remember
          when he leans his head back
and I can see the beat of the artery
          in his neck, this is what I hear
when I listen to the light
          pulsing on his skin.

# Epistrophy

The sleeve sighs from the jacket,
        the record from the sleeve.
The needle takes its breath.

I know what's next—
        the horns, the hymns
that spiral back to silence

after the room fills with the sound
        of another room, the sound
of steel as it fills the groove.

Tonight it's *Monk's Music*, a record
        that begins in evening
and then turns back to twilight.

It pleads, "Abide with Me,"
        and then demurs, "Well,
You Needn't," as dark rewinds.

Halfway back to "Crepuscule,"
        it stops to ask
for another hand, and I have to rise

to turn the record as the room
        remembers the room it used to be.
I have to raise the needle

I couldn't touch, once
        too delicate for my hand,
needle that had to wait

for my father's. He'd stand
        some nights in silence,
smoke his only word, then reach

and take the arm. Or he'd stand
        and take a breath—
sigh of the sleeve in the jacket—

cough the door and be gone.
        Like those movies,
like those nightclub films

where Monk stands from the piano,
        turns his quiet waltz,
then walks off the stand,

twenty, thirty minutes gone,
        the sidemen keeping time
while he works the night shift

at the furnace, I have to wait
        for morning or evening again
to hear the other side,

Monk has to stay
        in his child-red wagon,
while the stars spin through the pines.

Now, I turn the music back,
        turn it over, as light eases
back into the sky. Dad

wakes the blanket, the amp,
        the smell of solder, smell
of oil instead of iron, twilight

instead of twilight. Then
        the room is young again,
the smoke, the silence, the stars,

years away, until dusk
        raises its hands from the keys.
Then the needle gasps,

and I stand. I reach,
        his hand on mine,
and breathe again.

# Letter to Be Wrapped around
## a 12-Inch Disc

*—To Major Jackson, from Gadsden, Alabama*

Here it is, first disc I remember

     pulling from the bin—jacket
white, label a dish of radio waves,
       the way I wished

I could have seen the world, the sky
      those nights when I pressed my ear
to the speakers and dialed the tuner

      through Birmingham,
Jackson, New Orleans, reaching
     for the sound of some beyond,

praying each night not only
     not to die

but to wake up and discover
     what I'd always known, myself
an alien with this second sight,

     the world a book
of such vibration I could see
     what I needed. And I needed

this, this music, whosoever it was,
     this elsewhere
I pulled from its sleeve and spun

beneath the needle, this orchestra
crash, this rush, this planet rocked
                with lasers

like the blasts we hammered
            out of high-tension wires,

a strange music at last
                    near at hand.

Each one was a rocket taking off,
            not landing, which is what

I prayed against each night
                the shells flashed
on the army range a few hills distant

        which we knew would be
among the first to go if
                the Russians struck,

everything we knew turned first
            to light and then to ash . . .

I can hear it now, lightning crack
                in the Memphis channel,

*hit me*, in Bambaataa's spin,
        Bambaataa's beat, the shock

of doors opening between the stars,

            of someone reaching
down, George Clinton or Jesus
        Christ, someone reaching up,

Sun Ra's Rocket #9 taking off
             for Venus,

anywhere but this before
             the *radiation, mutation*
came down. I needed this,

                   this liberation music
I'd spin each night and sometimes
             cut the sound to listen

to the needle rattle in the groove,
                   a cicada in its shell,
waiting for wings to unfold,

             four dollars of polyrhythm,
of syncopation

                   to begin to hear
myself over the drawl of home

             and step to the mall-fountain
rap battles my friend coaxed me into,

                   teaching me
to fold a sentence
             to a hawk, a panther,
a rattlesnake, a rocket,
                   an origami star,

Southside hicks against
             boys from Litchfield
and Tuscaloosa Ave

I might see
in a parking lot
        pulling their moms to the curb

then dialing up the beat
                where we'd catch
each other's bob, a byword

        we needed to call across
the lines the county drew around us.

        We had so much
behind us, the history

        we were told we shouldn't
name, stir up, remember,
                so much silence

we needed to break. Alone
        and then together and then
alone again, because they told us

        we were young
and we should turn that noise down,

        we slid the discs off our fingers
until even the ridges of our prints
                felt musical.

Dap is the vibe passing
        hand to hand, hand to pen,
pen rolling like the needle

        over the dark

then pulling back to spin
      free again, so

fingerprints give up
         their songs,

and there in the dust
      of having met, Birmingham
drifts with Philly, New York
         with New Orleans.

Each note pops like lightning
      in the broadcast air,

like Robert Johnson's calloused
         palps on the steel

as he learned his graveyard music
      in a ghost town in Alabama
while looking up at the stars.

         Take this then
and spin it, pulling history
      back against itself until

you find the star-calling riff
         and everything falls

and elsewhere gives way
      to where and we don't have to
look away again.

         I fold the liner now,
my inked fingers leaving
      their rings here where

you will have to peel the tape
                    to open the disc
of night to set it reeling,

            in its grooves the plosive novas
of dust, the afterwards of skin
                    dropping

new beats between
            the ones we already know.

## Letter Hidden in a Letter to Cy Twombly

I dreamed I was blind

       but could make a word
by curling a strand of hair
           into letters,

one at a time. I prayed
       the scales would fall.

At night, I waited for the river's
          sentence to unfold,

a tale of snake handlers, the gift
       of all living tongues.

I could write with a tooth,
          the pencil's other end,

regardless of day, could etch
       my poem, salt into windowglass.

Somewhere the lost boat's gone
         mineral, petrified

in starlight without a bone

      to autograph. Just
one letter in a strand of code.

        Given the right oblivion,
one hand can remember another,

but tonight, the river
manages only the bark of leather

on stone, clap
of footpalms on the bank,

its one strand curling

a word no one's slow enough
to read.

# Postscript

For Medgar Evers

I didn't want to write this,
even to think of you,
afraid the thought would curl,
would tangle and make you
common and factual as light.
So I've waited,
hands, pencils down.
Now that seems a prayer
against the world and being in it.
That is why he waited
in the bushes. That is a prayer
the closed eyes say.
This is not the afterimage
but the image of day
on paper, in its pores,
new light that shows the edges,
so nothing can be hid,
even if the words curl like hair,
even if they curl like vine.
Again, today, the light is new,
and because you are nowhere
you are everywhere,
in the face of which I'd ask
how can I say anything,
in the face of which I ask
how can I say nothing at all?

# Mayflower

For John Earl Reese, a sixteen-year-old, shot by Klansmen
through the window of a café in Mayflower, Texas, where he
was dancing, October 22, 1955

Before the bird's song
you hear its quiet

which becomes part of the song
and lives on after,

struck notes bright
in silence

as the room's damp—
wallpaper and wall

muffling the high cicadas'
whine, mumbling

talk from another room—
hangs like the thought

of a roof in the midst of rain
long after the joists

have been brought down.
So the quiet

syllables crowded
full throats once the talkers

have gone away,
and a young man's voice

becomes a young man's
silence, all

he did not say,
which nothing keeps

saying in the empty room
between the pines

that hold the quiet
of the song he cannot sing,

the sound of a room
without sound

in the middle of what
anyone can hear.

# Letter Written on a
# Hundred Dollar Bill

*—To Howlin' Wolf, from Mississippi*

Did your right hand itch when I transcribed your O
*don't you hear me cryin?* phrase I'd pay a hundred dollars
to raise my voice into, cause you got money for sure,
not like Son House in the nightclub film, drunk
as a goat glutted with rotten apples and waving a sawbuck
like a flag, but stacking up in a New York office
like a locomotive's chimney if I keep this going
and then I imagine raining down into the world below
or uncurling on a magnolia only you know
how to find, my hundred plucked, still crisp,
then rolled up in your pocket as you walk again
from White Station and West Point to Grenada,
Ruleville, Rosedale with a guitar on your back,
where you meet Charley Patton again.
You pull out the bankroll and count off a Cadillac
so y'all can cruise to Memphis, St. Louis, Chicago,
unpack at the 708 or Silvio's and maybe House
is already there at the bar, rediscovered
and thirsty for oblivion, when Sumlin walks in
with Dixon and you're ready to pitch it again,
and the microphones are humming so you can invent
rock and roll or whatever it is Eric Clapton
tries to play in that London session when you take over,
showing him that music is a kind of language,
you just say this, you just call roosters and cats
and airplane pilots into the club, the whole
Wang Dang Doodle of the afterlife catching your notes
like undampered pianos and sounding long after
you've gone down the blue highways back to Jackson,

Nashville, Lebanon where your girl stands in the door
of the house you kept together as peaceful and bright
as the day you met, you're gathering everyone you know
and rolling down to Natchez where the fire
hasn't ashed the Rhythm Club and the whole town's
waiting for you to take the stage, maybe costumed
like an engineer or busking like a janitor,
the mic taped to a broom handle, the sheet-metal walls
shaking when you let out your O,
O there is no sound like this in the world above
except the one you engraved in the great disc of the night
that spins above us, through the hole of which
every C-note floats to bud from that one magnolia
somewhere in east Mississippi where this sound was born.
When you walk down the dirt roads each night,
when you pull your hands from your pockets, the lint
turns everything first-spring green,
and when you open your song you light the underworld
with a throat and a mouth full of gold.

# Letter Written on a Record Sleeve

*—To Jason Moran*

Pulled from the jacket, puckered,
      slipped from its lacquer disc,
it's just a twelve-inch square, an envelope
          waiting for something to hold,

just a blank piece of paper
      I've had since I was twelve
and I slid *Planet Rock* from a bargain bin
        at the Gadsden Mall

because of a name I couldn't say.
      Dubbed, it was a four-dollar soundtrack
to lying in the yard and waiting
        for the swift point of a satellite

to scratch the drawn geometries
      and break free. . . .
Somewhere between the stars
        was a song I hadn't heard,

maybe waiting on a gold LP,
      like Voyager's, to be spun,
somewhere past Jupiter
        which we'd seen on TV,

its color waiting folded in the dark
      for any passing eye.
Afternoons, decades of hot light,
        centuries had faded everything

dull as the Hank Jr. tape
        stuck in my father's deck
so I'd dream it mumbling in static
            past New Orleans or Houston

coming in clearer after sundown,
        and maybe you were listening, too,
your hands ready for Monk's
          percussive touch,

barrelhouse stomp forgotten
        then uttered as a new idea,
fresh rhythm bouncing
         the ionosphere.

The paper can make that sound,
        crack of dust beneath the stylus,
and laid on the Steinway's low strings
          catch the hammer

your beat hand makes.
        It rattles, a recording
of the heart played back
         through a busted amp,

a sock full of silver dollars
        dropped beside the bed.
My mom said her grandfather kept them,
         one for each rocket,

Mercury 3 to Apollo 10,
        and the flight he'd waited for,
the broadcast he'd miss,
         man walking on the moon,

who'd cut farm from forest,
              from hoe cough to AM radio
and color TV, how he watched
              the stars and waited,

which is why they'd let me
              fall asleep in the yard. . . .
Maybe I can go back now,
              the dew

just about to bead, moon to curl
              itself into those lenses,
blades about to flower
              new constellations

in answer to the night
              while the headphones pulse
their binary and theremin sine,
              maybe I can go back

while space troughs in the acre's
              old terraces, and I can
lean down and change the tape
              so Blind Willie Johnson's

"Dark Was the Night, Cold
              Was the Ground" can unreel . . .
it could rise from the earth,
              old language, or fall

from the gold record spinning
              somewhere between the stars
where all the words
              have gone to melody.

And you . . . wherever you are tonight,
       reach into the dark and key
the figure, the record sleeve
           tucked in the bass-clef strings

so the beat sounds like a memory
       of the heart played back
at a distance, through static
         and years and wind.

It reaches back, like the future,
       which is just another kind
of history, a shape
         for whatever's missing

that fills its own outlines in.

# Abide

Cloudless, birdless, twilight's
blur, a gray somewhere

between the lacquer and the keys,
the piano's black pearled

on your fingernails,
the small half dark,

the "Crepuscule" the hands
stroll together when the legs cannot,

the smell of brass and wood
warming half-time

beneath rosemary and cream and wine
I'm easing toward the plates.

Half rest, whole, the chord
my great-grandmother's kitchen,

its steam of greens, stew of tomato
and okra and sheet music's cedar,

cooked cabbage worn home
from the teacher's house,

her hands slicing the onion thin,
the left hand, the right,

the upright's wood I must hum
after supper already moving,

your hands musical
in the half-remembered parlor,

walking in mine, my hands
working with a strength

only half,
only twice my own.

# Postscript Written on a J-Card

Of course,
my mother had two grandfathers

who were both stories by the time
I was born,

memories passed like plates at holiday tables.

Like my grandmother's recipes,
you'd get the idea
but not the numbers.

So one great-grandfather built the house
where we'd gather,

perfect plumb,
tornado-strong,

where I'd listen, trying

to piece it all together, there

on the remnant of the farm, twelve
broad acres of grass and the few

pecans' arthritic hands on the crest
of the hill he cut from the forest,

leaving three houses, his fields' terraces,
and a purse of silver dollars.

The other one is also a shadow
        I see from behind
                        in vignettes of history,

easy-chaired and turned
            toward a radio, a television,

listening to, watching each space shot,

        and telling my mom,
                        *I started out in a buggy,*

*horse-drawn buckboard, and have seen*
            *the car, the plane, the rocket . . .*

how he wanted to see a man walk
        on the moon before he died.

There are all these silver dollars,
            sometimes spread on the table

after the plates are cleared
        and touched, broke

mnemonics that summon one line
        of a story but not

another, the years remembering the cotton mills,
        the three wars, the gradual thinning

of the stars. This was the town
        with the first electric

street lights, or so we were told,

                the town where the army kept
its first chemical weapons, so the memories are

                gasses, or vapor lights

switching on and off,

                        and when
        this ravel of family is done,

the dollars would be stacked
                and gathered again. Now

I have this purse and its coins and bits of story
                that don't fit together. So

I do the one thing the farm taught me
                and look away,

                        into the stars
and try to shape the dots
        into myths. Poems are made,

Levis said, by forgetting,
                *the only kind of forgetting*

*which is also a form of remembering.*

        I lie down in the grass again.

As the song fades out there's a second
                or two of tape that sounds like

someone talking into a pillow,
        conversation heard through a wall,

which I'd figured
             was the TV bleeding,

caught by the needle when I made my dub.

             It must continue, beneath the music,
whatever show my dad was watching,

                    and in years of looping the tape
I might have memorized the rhythm

       of *Hee Haw* or *Mork & Mindy*
or Reagan one January night

       telling everyone *Nothing ends here.*

Somewhere in the great ecliptic,
             the two grandfathers become one,

the stars, the lines from one story
       wrapping with another's.

So many people tangle there,

             their names, their stories
becoming one another's.

       Spaceman, listener, grandfather, cousin,

reach down and fill this case
             with stars.

# Exploded View

While he slept, I read my father's books
brought home from the furnace,
traced the diagrams—channels, ladles of iron,

oxygen lances—trying to follow
the metal's path, to follow the work
that took him each night into the dark—

flame to the coal's dark, the dark
gone bright while the rest of us slept.
The door closed like a storybook. . . .

While he worked, the furnace flamed
in dream, and I tried to follow
through the swarm of yellowjackets,

hot wings of iron, but they were just
outlines in my dream, dream,
not iron, not fire in the dark—just spray

from one rare story I tried to follow.
I tried to follow, but even he
didn't want to go, not even

in story, the blanks in the books'
diagrams all ash, all flame. All silence,
they seemed to say. But silence

is a furnace, too, where work
disappears, where breath is turned
to iron. And night is a furnace, too,

where sleep, where dark are burned away
like words until the books are blank
and there's nothing left to follow.

I tried, listening as he eased the stairs,
clicked the door, then drove away,
his engine lost in the trains' low drone,

strained to hear him turning,
ten miles away, pages in the book of iron,
the story he told by not telling,

the dark in which the furnace always rests.
So, the furnace is a father, too,
whose story you cannot follow,

a shadow sitting loud in the dark,
while the quiet hardens in his lungs.

And the father is a story, too,
you cannot follow,
a book fed slowly to the fire,

a fire, worked, at last,
to two black tongues of iron.

# My Great-Grandmother's Snuff Cup

When she raised the cup
the dark slid into, not from,
the dark slid from her lip
as if she ate the morning paper
with her eggs, every *she said*
thrilled her pulsing gums,
every *she said* a hornet swarming
the day-moon's skull
or flushed from twilight caves
to bat overhead
like minnows in a spring,
the world turned upside down.
This is how her stillborn fell out
and rolled over the ridge
to live with those bitches,
the ones with turtles
snapped to their teats, the ones
who eat the scabs from their faces,
who chew until the color's gone
out of even their dreams
and their teeth fall out because
that is what happens
when you let your family go,
when you walk off and live
alone, you have nothing,
and nothing else to eat but you.

# Feedback Loop

The chair, the bedside tables,
the TV stand come out

after she does, and then
the bed, each thing leaving

its weight in the rugs,
as if you'd erased these letters

carefully, leaving blanks
sharp as words. As if

I could erase her voice
from this cassette and listen

to her quiet open and close.
Carpet bright below the sills.

A memory of breath
heard beneath the door.

Maybe ghosts
don't want to come back.

Maybe we keep saying
their silences between our words,

the shape of their voices
in ours, in ours

the warmth that haunts
their absent lungs.

# Letter Written in Black Water
# and Pearl

*—To Yusef Komunyakaa*


When I rise from the bank
the water's slow as shadow
in my steps, thick as blood.
The whole river's secretive,
still, dark as roux
cooled in the skillet, as rank,
as sweet, ancient as catfish,
ancienter. The moon's
sifted light clouds rumor
to lilies or daffodils,
an egret on the farther shore,
a hunger, a stare, a patience
I could recite. We have
waited all night, nights,
like a bridge for something
to rise, like water
for something to fall.

\*


I know what Bogalusa means,
that tea of deadheads
and late-fallen leaves
no one left can read,
snuff-black pools that bathe
grandmothers' gums.
So many words one has
to know not to say.
So many names. The young,
unconvicted hand. The brick-

layer. The deputy. Names
of flowers and warblers and stars.
Last breaths of the disappeared.
I keep my hands folded,
my map blank
as next week's papers,
my ears clams
with mouths full of sand.

*

So many songs I can't sing
with my one poor tongue.
I need a jukebox for a throat
so the midnight's moan
translates what a wolf
once said to a girl in the trees,
so their branches confess
what the fog told them not
to see. I need the lisp
of a horn valved to spit,
which is the sound of a shadow
forgetting what hanged it
in the dark. How do I explain
the way it slips the steam
like a shirt, how it slides
beneath the glass and does not
rise again, how the half-light
fingers the rails of the bridge,
how many things
no one's done?

*

Birds the color of history
talk in our sleep. Our salts
can't forget what water
told them, what stars

once telegraphed to the river
the trees have written
in themselves, what they say
to the wind, to the saw-
mill's blades, to flame,
to bromine and mercury,
what they burn in the air.
Dreams walk us back
to the shore, pull the shirttail
from the milkweed, the cattail
from the reed, fold
the kerchiefs into herons,
questions for the shoals.

*

Night slips again
into its last, locked groove.
Mockingbirds stutter
the rasp of broken reeds.
I lean from the eaves
of moss and cypress,
the vestibules of the tung.
Cormorant, coelacanth, snake,
the world below is molten.
Dark iridescence,
the muscle gives back the bone.
The spine's fleer, the orbits'
gape, the ghost of a face
waking beneath my own.
Here, I bent so close
breath didn't know
which mouth to fill.

# Laws of Conservation

Does the river, after
it's come apart,
still hold the drowned
hand's tremble, still
reach for sky or branch
or oar? Delicate sweat
of a delicate hand,
tease of hair before
the rope makes its fist—
music, time, whiskey
flower and decay.
Night is an open mouth.
Breath minnows the water,
whispers leaves as if
through lace
to some forbidden ear.
Maybe the trees
remember that fruit,
the water its dew-
washed down. Maybe
water could return
that skin's last itch
to the lips that glisten
behind the ear.
Wish of every silence,
every sigh, breath
that's passed, that's
passing—that pleasure
hangs forever.
Memory, is anything
this cruel?

# Cry of the Occasion

For John Earl Reese, shot while dancing in a café in
Mayflower, Texas, October 22, 1955

so loud it fills the valleys
of even the fingers smeared
into a kind of quiet, the everything
you can't hear but hear through
the music every body in the room
still moving the beat gone erratic as a bat
juking the pines and chimney
swifts toward grace notes
of nourishment over the lake
I see in the perpetual lapping of water
in the lock groove of some cousin's
record I put my finger to
pull back the arm but it shivers
toward the moon thrown like a penny
from the engine's wheel like the sound
of a penny thrown from the glass
calling my name louder than I've ever
heard this part before a bird
whose name's so long
it has never finished saying it
holds me waiting for the end so I
can say something a little more blunt
like thunder a finger through the bone
peeling back the husk of the voice
opening like a bird called into
the wild answering but
like the bird I have not even seen

this music goes on forever the stars
blur the bottleneck against the bridge
swallows abandon for the water
cutting into the bank where I keep
trying to move the needle
to cut my answer into the night
I have to catch the bird and slide it
against my neck I have to carve
the guitar from the deadheads beneath
the lake and all its waves to sing

# The Voice of Woody Guthrie Wakes in an Antenna in Okemah, Oklahoma

They have painted me
　　　　on a building—steel strings
strung out into concrete
　　　　　　　and air
　　　　beneath a palomino's thunder—
and cast me in bronze or copper
　　　　or something like that
and set me in an empty lot
　　　　　　　two blocks
　　　　from where I was born

so I am always here
　　　　in this old, dark town

but the voice is waking up
　　　　　　　out of
　　　　an old 78 somewhere
in New York and out of
　　　　magnetic tape in Washington
and stars and switches in Oregon
　　　　　　　or California,

　　　　it spreads out on a wave
from Oklahoma City
　　　　to coalesce again on the tower
on the fire station's roof
　　　　　　　where I could see
　　　　Warn's Furniture and the library,
the cemetery and the Canadian
　　　　River winding west

and south of town. The whole night
                is a trembling sound

        and even songs I'd only sung
with my pen come back to settle
                in the voice, so this land
is your land and this town
                        is your old, dark town,

        the Oklahoma Hills
are yours, the oak and the blackjack
                and the kiss of sand or black
dust in the prairie wind,
                yours as well, so you will

remember the childhood drugstore
                        postcard photograph
        though it was not your childhood

it is now, you will remember
                the scene, your father will have
told you he was there and you may be
                        able to pick him out
                of the crowd on the bridge
over the river, over the bodies
                that pull down those ropes
taut as big fiddle strings
                        you can hear when
        the wind blows or the hand,
the right hand comes down
                on the dreadnaught's E,

you will remember it, even
                        without hands
        you can hold the postcard

to the air, right over the place
        as the trembling night puts the words
in the filament in your throat, pulsing
                first as typewriter's
        keys and then as nerves
that shape the muscles that shape
        the wind, *It showed the Canadian*

*River Bridge / Three bodies hanging*
                *to swing in the wind /*
        *A mother and two sons they'd lynched*

though the postcard has just one
        son, one mother, even

without hands you can hold
                the photograph to the air
        right over the place and see
the prairie rolling south toward
        Texas, the sodium glow
of Wetumka and Tupelo campfires
                on the curve, and
        if you wait long enough, until

the sun begins to wake the salt
        in the morning air, there,
where Durant would be, another
                photograph, another
        body hung from a tree,
another postcard taken just before
        they take the body down

and set it ablaze, and if you wait
                long enough, you'll see
        that black tornado of smoke

gathering overhead and blowing here
        the last words of John Lee,

you'll hear them cross the last words
        of Lawrence and Laura Nelson
hanged just three months earlier
                in the childhood photograph
        that shows everything but

the baby, Laura's baby, the one thing
        they did not hang,
which must be crying somewhere,
                and then you will understand
        the second son in the song
the night remembers to your throat

        is the cry of the child
that doesn't die there, the cry that stays
                and slowly lathes itself
        into the picture, the cry

that calls John Lee the hundred miles over
        the prairie to be here in the scene
you see from the signal tower
                on the firehouse
        in downtown Okemah,

and you will see, as the morning pulls
        the song from your throat,
as you scan the horizon, Ada,
                Anadarko, Tulsa,
        all the photographs still hung

over their places in the air,
        you will hear all those last words

still trembling, even without statues,
                    and this town
        will be your town, these words

will be your words. You will never
        stop saying them.

Their wind will be your wind.


                                        *for Brian Barker*

# Letter from Okemah

*. . . this is the reckoning I claim . . .*
—Terrance Hayes

A photograph let hang
a century, Oklahoma
fades into Oklahoma,
the road ahead, the whole horizon

beaten to a brass forever
soon we'll rapture up,
curving almost noticeably,
to melt into that metal.

The next word we see
should be the name of God,
but *Okemah*'s just another town,
two miles closer to the sun.

I know this name,
inked on a photograph
as brown and bright as afternoon
and again and again on postcards

and in your poem which says itself
to me. If I close my eyes
I can see it, the Canadian River,
five miles west. I can see her,

print dress over the water,
Laura Nelson, feet floating free.
And if I look at her, then look away,
if I say the name the picture has erased

and do not look at the locals or the bridge
where light has knit the rope into the sun
and do not turn to see her son,
half naked, Lawrence, on the line,

I can see her flying from the water
into indefinite afternoon.
But I see them, I see them all,
and cannot look away.

They're all there, the photograph
hung over its place in the air
rippling in the heat as in the bath
where the page first learned it,

water I want to break
to steal the light that burns her there,
her son's light, too, and leave
the townsfolk where their gaze

can dry the river to a trace,
in a bright that will not blink
until they're burnt back to salt,
to terror's silk, to paper.

But that time has become a place
light cannot move.
*Okemah* means *things up high*.
Say it, and the bridge is there,

the town, the cottonwoods, the frame
in a faded parlor that holds this scene,
the curtains moths have laced,
tassels waiting for latent hands,

the sound horn of the gramophone
where I hinge the needle into the groove
of a hundred years' sound
and finger the platen's edge

and pull it back
until the horn is gasping,
until the sound's gone out of everything
and the wind is coming in.

# Postscript to Silence

After the palm has clasped the hot, white
iron, the pain whispers slow
as the march of torches up the ridge.
Perverse lava, flowing up,
pine knots flicker their shirts, their hoods,
white as eschar. You hear
the crackle, the whip, later on.
Here, lips part but make no sound.
Words suppurate slowly, halving
then halving their distance to your ears,
moving like bees in a cry of amber.
How old will you be when they arrive,
when you remember the tissue
your mother brought to her tears,
watching the fire climb through the window,
how white it was, when you remember
the sound of what you did not hear?
That's when you'll feel the burn,
when you'll feel the shape of those words,
even the ones she could not say.

# Letter Already Broadcast into Space

*—To Sun Ra, from Earth*


You are not here,

you are not here
                in Birmingham,
        where they keep your name,

not in Elmwood's famous plots
                or the monuments
of bronze or steel or the strew

        of change in the fountain
where the fire hoses sprayed.

                In the furnaces,
in the interchange sprawl
        that covers Tuxedo Junction,

in the shopping malls
                they've forgotten you,

the broadcast towers, the barbecues,

        the statue of the Roman god,
spiculum blotting out
                part of the stars.

To get it dark enough,
        I have to fold back
into the hills, into the trees

where my parents
planted me, where the TV
    barely reaches and I drift

with my hand on the dial
    of my father's radio,

spinning, too, the tall antenna
    he raised above the pines.

I have to stand at the base

    of the galvanized
pole I can use as an azimuth
    and plot you in.

The hunter's belt is slung again,
    and you are there

in the pulse, in the light of
    Alnitak, Alnilam, Mintaka,

all your different names,

    you are there
in all the rearrangements
    of the stars.

    Come down now,
come down again,

    like the late fall light
into the mounds along the creek,

light that soaks like a flood
to show the Cherokee sitting upright
                underground, light

like the fire they imply.

        Come down now
into the crease the freight train
                hits like a piano's hammer

and make the granite hum
        beneath.

                Come down now

as my hand slips from the dial,
                tired again of looking
for the sound of another way

        to say everything.

Come down now with your diction
                and your dictionary.

Come down now like the stars
        and help me rise.

I have forgot my wings.

# Abide

Forgive me if I forget
with the birdsong and the day's
last glow folding into the hands
of the trees, forgive me the few
syllables of the autumn crickets,
the year's last firefly winking
like a penny in the shoulder's weeds,
if I forget the hour, if I forget
the day as the evening star
pours out its whiskey over the gravel
and asphalt I've walked
for years alone, if I startle
when you put your hand in mine,
if I wonder how long your light
has taken to reach me here.

# Letter Written in the Breath

*—To Kerry James Marshall, from Birmingham*

Nothing will be this white,

      white that sees you looking
and says *look away,*

        so, soften, blue
from powdered cadmium,

      one grain strong enough
to darken a lung

        so you hold
your breath while the knife
     and the brush

tell it what to do. First,

        coffee's steam,
broad veins thinning, sun's
      cream blown into the disc

until it's cool enough to drink.

       So, the iris
into the eyewhite, then

      blast-furnace gas,
hand-me-down chambray,

cyanotype portraits
fading to nightclub smoke,
        predawn blur,

Polaroid lilacs drying
            in a grandmother's vase—

parlor, ceiling, mirror, ether—

        the hair offering
its color to cotton, to linen,

            to suggest jacquard
and the wallpaper's flock,
        requiem beveled into glass,

scabbards of gladiolas, roses
            on all the tables,

these rooms in L.A.
        or Chicago or Birmingham—

the hair offering its color
            to the cloth, the reed

its fray to the column of air.

    *Alabama, Alabama,*
Coltrane says, and Baraka muses
            in the notes,

*I didn't realize until now*
        *what a beautiful* word
*Alabama is.* . . .

Movement's caught,
stillness kept in these rooms,

the way you replay a tune
or a sermon you've heard
so many times

you know each syllable, each
motion, it never goes

away. Time is moving forward
in memory, memory's

moving back, Trane thinking
Birmingham, reading the paper

where King has said *This afternoon*
*we gather*
*in the quiet of this sanctuary,*

Trane takes his breath,
air through the feathers
of the throat,

lost in the cymbals' brass,
this breath, their breath, these girls—

*Addie Mae, Denise, Carole, Cynthia—*

breath their parents' took,
breath they held—

Birmingham's, where

we learned to breathe

—and what comes out
          is rooms, each

with the banner, the souvenir,
          the three portraits,

Kennedy, King, and Kennedy,
          and the black-letter prayer

                    *We Mourn Our Loss,*

but there is more than this

          because breath is a house,
breath is a city,

          the smoke of each gun,
each bomb or burning car
          still there, each gasp, so

what comes out is portraits,
          the girls' faces,
wreathed in the wings,

          what comes out is Medgar Evers
and Jimmie Lee Jackson, Chaney,
          Goodman, and Schwerner,

and what comes out is Viola Liuzzo,
          Mark Clark, Fred Hampton
and Malcolm X,

          what comes out
is Trane calling Roy Hamilton
          into heaven, Skip James

to Coleman Hawkins
        through the gates

because we carry part
        of Christ's breath in our breath,

the breath what remains.

        So memory's fog
is the breath on the mirror's glass,

    the breath, not the glass,

all speech, all inscriptions visible,
          what's written in air,

all the rooms.

        And nothing there's
as white as white's first syllable,

nothing gold as the wings
        memory unfolds.

Nothing's as still, nothing
      as quick as this time that lapses,

as the time
      that always remains.

# Inscription for Air

For John Earl Reese, shot while dancing in a café in
Mayflower, Texas, October 22, 1955

Not for the wound, not for the bullet,
     power's pale cowardice, but
for you, for the three full syllables
     of your name we hold whole
as a newborn by the feet, and so
     for the cry, the first note, the key
of every word to follow, the timbre,
     the tone, the voice that could sing
Nat King Cole's "If I May," and slow-
     dance the flipside, the blossoms
fallen like a verdict to the jury's lips,
     not to the blood or the broken
glass or the spider's silking juke-
     box wires in a junkman's shed,
but the fingers' heat still on the dime
     when it slides to the switch,
the lamp on the platter, the groove
     that tells the needle what to say,
and the pine boards of the café floor
     once moved by the locusts' moan
now warm as a guitar's wood, revived
     with all the prayers of song, *Amens*
that flame when a blues turns bright,
     not for what was lost, but what
was lived, what is written here,
     in the night, in vinyl, in the air,

for the bead of sweat at the hair's deckle,
      the evening star in the trees,
soda pop sugar wild on your tongue and
      for the tongue telling Saturday night
something of Sunday morning, fluent
      as a mockingbird, and for the hand
that opens as if in praise, as if in prayer,
      asking for another to fill it there,
for the smile and for the smile of skin
      behind the ear where love might lip its name,
for you, if we may, pull back the arm
      and start this music once again.

# Dear Brother,

Hank Williams dreams the unknown grave of Rufus Payne

You can keep on knocking
      but you can't

make a sound. The door's
      been torn and only

a hole's been left in the frame,
      the sound of one hand

keeping time against the air.
      Keep on till the knothole

or the bung falls out and all
      the beer, all the spirit

spills to the ground, for all those
      who can't be here anymore.

Come Tee-Tot, come teeter
      ridgepole and spine

to watch the crawdads scumble
      in the mud, riverboats

knocked slow in the river's groove,
      scuttles wider

than the mouth on a 45
      or a gun or a whiskey bottle

that only spills out tea.
        Keep on knocking

till the roof falls open,
        a song as old as anyone alive

shambled off the edge of a dime
        on a doorstep in Georgiana

to my own once-shy ears.
        Come home, Tee-Tot,

come and answer the door,
        the chimney, this hailstorm

of singles with that Storyville
        song once spilled

from the holes
        in Jelly Roll's face.

Shut me up with the bucket
        and the washboard and the harp

and the cymbals on your knees,
        then set me to sing again.

Come home, dear brother,
        or tell me where

to meet you in that city
        where there is no pain.

# Tape Loop

touch the lip so silence
has a name neither of us
can pronounce
on midnight radio from Memphis
Houston Phoenix a beat
rattling in the valley
like the needle I am not
supposed to touch
between the trees in those
country songs my prayer
a sound that doesn't play
in this town I am
not supposed to click the button
so this gets dubbed
onto the ribbon in the black
cassette that gets dubbed
onto the ribbon in the white
cassette as the needle drops
the beat the head says
this town is a form of silence
waiting for the drum
of the tongue the lip
the sentence we're stretching
when we make our bodies music
we make an elsewhere
whose name reaches
toward the center and the needle's
caught it when the beat
slows between the tracks

your voice my voice
our elsewhere music
the groove never knew
it couldn't touch

*for Collis Marchbanks*

# Letter Written in Someone Else's Hand

*—To Natasha Trethewey, from Atlanta*

You see it first—the cut
      eye, tensed lip, the craned
body's English you read so well,

        the eyewhite's question
for anything not white as bone.
      Once the napkins furl,

once the wine is poured, you lean
        to ask, sly and quiet,
*Did we just integrate this place?*

      The tea lights laugh with us,
antique shadow, antique flame,
        recalling before the arson,

the cleansing fire, before the phoenix,
      cannon and tallow in the markets,
fingers in the hair, on the gums,

        fingers held for the nails
to be read, the moons, you tell us,
      once thought blood's tattoo.

Now, our hands are splayed,
        each phase—last, half,
gibbous—clear as you reach

and spin our histories out of us.
You smile, the punch line quiet,
                my quarters waxing bright

in your palm, and the candles
                and the table laugh again. Now
the sepias, the tintypes my grandmother's

                grandmother walked out of,
from the Cherokee mountains into
                Alabama to wed a paler name,

the dimes she spent on the town's
                fairest girls while her daughters
worked the mill's second shift,

                my grandmother's, my mother's
once long black hair—all seem
                at once so faint, and still

so clear. Later, I know, we'll stand
                outside and pass the joke again,
washed together in streetlight and moon-

                light, in headlamps and glare,
as we pass into each other's stories.
                In evening's last embraces,

we'll learn again the warmth of each
                other's blood. We'll feel it
slip into the night, into the dark

                each pulse engraves, as we pull
our fingers across each other's, back
                against the grain.

# Letter Written in the Dark

*—To Cy Twombly*

Shinbone, Dirtseller, Sleeping Giants—

      dream phrases, names
memory's made illegible,

      the notes I find are written over one another,

tangled as the hair a pillow offers afternoon.

      Shenandoah, Three Sisters, Tobacco Row—
this is what the blind hand writes in the dark.

      Scallop of uplift, scales wind can hammer
into river or sea.

      Last night someone sprayed
      every slur they knew

on the piers beneath the bridge
      where schoolkids pass their bottle

with only the current to tell them hush.

      Last call drifted
through the window from the street below,

      one last Negroni, last coin

turned to doo-wop on the juke,
      and you dreamed of music

you don't even like—*Please, please, don't go . . .*

       —a radio pouring its water into a room
you've almost forgot.

               Static of pines,
         the frosting window's crackle,

tomorrow will wash it into clouds,

      bright silences you might pass,
months later, wondering how the words

         come to your lips,

*Ophiuchus, Sagitta, Lyre,*

            faint as constellations
     someone's erased onto the walls

of a rented room. The lines, in twilight,
        the names rise from the walls.

All night, the night remembers the shapes to the window,
     each erasure doubled, but one

that would graze into the frame if night held on,

        one the sun keeps,
the window, the earth, one even the walls

    have never seen, which gives that pencil's end

a month in which to work. Soon,
        the Lyre will spill its music,

Hermes to Apollo to Orpheus,

      a story that almost recites itself—

the tortoise pulled from the water,
          slain to hold those songs

of light, passed down, dropped

      back into wine-dark or iron-bright water,

then raised into the night to fall
          through the middle of every spring.

In the white each meteor etches,
       the perfection of marble, mineral forever

quarried from the blinding noon
         of the sea,

the hand knows the faint lines
       of graphite, the cinders of prayer

a poet has laid for a brother he can't see home,

        thin paraphs of the sailor's eyes
before they're scabbed by rime.

     *Say Goodbye Catullus, to the Shores of Asia Minor,*

and the fields, Phrygia and Troas and Nicea,
        say goodbye,

*linquantur* to liquid,
          vellum giving its atramentum back
to the cuttlefish and the octopi.

Weekends, in Augusta, you'd watch ink collect
                beneath a motel bed

and pool toward the chair, the curtains,

        then sprawl to let the right hand stray,

the squares of paper darkening fogs
                as the hand forgot its postures

and the Army's scrolls of code you'd turned
                back into poems and folk tales

and lines from popular songs—

        Orpheus on the banks of Isar singing
*the lonely day has flown my way,*

        or *the lovely day has flown away—*

beneath, some untutored cursive.

        So, in Rome, in Bolsena,

you furl the canvas on the floors
        and reach into the dark for its words,

into the hand.
                Water, water. Swimmer or skiff. Raft
        of the drowned man's body.

Sea spray or smoke. The burning ship.
        The lost canoe. Papyrela, limbus, pirogue.

Only the words come back.
                The Tiber lisps

in the Lungoteveri, trying to remember
      its name. The James

over its shoals. Starlight, streetlight
          finger the clouds. Waves

recite the absent moon—feldspar from basalt,
      salt from obsidian—

and one light remembers another.

        In the breath between the grasp
and the alpenglow, pencil and cinder and grease

    repair the boat to the shore,
the thought to its history,

      a pale Etruscan lime

that knows the water's autographs.

    Soon, morning will veil the window
and swallow all the letters

     and all the caves.

Only the river never turns from its poem.

      Sometimes you are there to write it down.

# Postscript
## (Already Breaking in Distant Echoes)

*—To Sun Ra, from Earth*

Other sun among other suns,

        clavinet wave
in the Moog sine of the stars,

      tell me, Uncle Elsewhere,

when I lift my prayer into the night,
        how far

does it have to go, how far back,
      Alnitak, a millennium,

or Vega, twenty years away,

       how long past
this future I await,
        and how old,

    if it returns, your music,
your answer, your wave?

      If you are there,

in the light, behind it, if
    you are there,

       tell me

how to turn the dial
           or the dish

or the tall antenna my father raised,

      tell me how

to turn my head to listen,

           and how, at last,

to tell the past from the future
           if they both arrive.

# Letter to Be Read by Furnace Light

*—To Terrance Hayes, from Gadsden, Alabama*

I am on the wrong street in the wrong part of town
following the chain of a poem in which the wrong music
is on the radio in all the imagined rooms,
and it isn't even a radio but a record player and the disc
is Son House's 1941 session and probably the label
should look like the harp in the mouth of the Stella
or the welds of a locomotive's wheels because
this is the music of steel, music
you'd burn down mountains for, music
heated past any man's ability to see,
to the bright of pure iron that will call your blood
from your veins, your breath from your lungs
so the iron is blown stronger than ever,
steel you could roll, steel you could spin
to a filament, a fiber brighter than pulpwood or cotton.
This is the music of a body quoting back the machine
and a body exceeding it—this is John Henry music
John Henry can't sing, so it's been handed down
from the rail and the steam case and the coffin,
this is wake-up music which has walked me back
to the Mississippi gallery near the place
where the dark birds gather in the lake-edge oaks,
birds the color of vinyl where Son House
hears the train before it comes, before Lomax knows,
before the microphone knows, and then
it's the locomotive's music I'd hear each night
before my father followed it to the furnace,
steel rails humming, the hot metal smell

handed down like music from that place
where everyone's blood is called
by the same hungry fire.
I am not going to say the furnace light falls
on everyone the same because we know
when Andrew Jackson or John Coffee watches
Tallaseehatchee burn it's the same fire but not
the same heat the Choctaw feel
and because this is the town
where Bunk Richardson swung from the railroad trellis,
where Bill Moore was shot on his integration walk,
the town where Miss Mary Hamilton insisted
that the court call her by her last name, too,
and this is the town split in two
by the murder of a preacher by a Klansman
and the murder of a storekeeper by a neighborhood teen
which is what I imagine my father and Red are talking about
this one night as the heat runs out
and the exhaust gas burns its ghostly blue over the furnace
dyeing everything deeper than the denim they wear against the fire
which they know may become the fire,
and this is what they're working out,
what my father repeats when he comes home
and I am still in bed, and this is how I take part
in this music, turning around them as the record turns
in the light of the quartz lock and Son House
puts his pulse into the strings and becomes a man
with a guitar and a locomotive, too, and the iron
rains to the hearth and the steel is blown blind
and in a further room is rolled and drawn
into these fine threads that hold the notes
when the right hand touches them,
so call it the wrong music or the wrong room
or even the wrong part of town,
but we know these geographies are melted

and cast back again, light and music,
which is mine because it is ours
when the train passes by with its run-out pulse
and the blue flame rises over the county
like the shirts we shoulder to keep the fire out
and the shirts we button to keep the fire in.

FOREWORD TO A
SUBSEQUENT READING

ACKNOWLEDGMENTS

# Foreword to a Subsequent Reading

*Abide* is a book made of two books, each written over and within the other.

One of these books advances the project I've been developing for almost a decade now—in *Murder Ballads* (2005), A *Murmuration of Starlings* (2008), and *Persons Unknown* (2010)—to elegize each of the martyrs of the civil rights movement. When the Civil Rights Memorial was erected in Montgomery in 1989, its marble table included the names of forty men, women, and children who were martyred between 1954 and 1968 as part of the freedom struggle. Over the past two decades, "forgotten" cases have come back into the light, writing more darkly the faint names in the company of martyrs. With each recounting, my project has expanded. It was always too big for one book. It is more complicated than a simple serial form, like a trilogy. It is the work of a life, both countless and one; one cannot predict how long it will take, but it will take as long as it will take. *Abide* continues, advances, even as it contains, as it remains.

To elegize the martyrs of the movement requires delicacy, requires reflection. For a white man to elegize men, women, and children, murdered by men whom I resembled, demographically, by men to whom I may be related or for whom I may be mistaken—for this man to elegize these martyrs requires hesitation, a stutter, a silence in which the ghosts of the murderers may be sloughed from my skin, even if only for a moment. In these moments of hesitation, these poems consider or enact the consideration of the necessary ethical questions—what does it mean to elegize, what does it mean to elegize martyrs, what does it mean to disturb the symmetries of the South's racial politics or its racial poetics?

The project has two strands, then, an elegiac and an ethical one. The elegiac, I now refer to as *Inscriptions for Air*: it includes much of the work of the previous volumes, and it requires the work of volumes to come. *Inscriptions for Air* is then a book without a single spine, without a single binding. My hope is that its presence in a larger body of work that asks not only questions of memory but also questions of life will suggest the necessary continuity and perpetuity of the work of memory. We visit memory sites, like the Civil Rights Memorial, but if memory lives only there, it isn't memory anymore. Memory lives in the breath we breathe, in the air we make together.

The ethical strand explores in part the right of the elegist to approach the moment of martyrdom or the lives almost erased there. As the work of elegy in this regard involves crossing the color line DuBois wrote about and which so many segregationists and murderers reinscribed, the ethical work also involves entering what the poet Édouard Glissant called *relation*—a space of improvised relationships, dialogue between self and other that recognizes but is not bound by historical hierarchies of race, culture, or class. In relation, self and other approach (or try to approach) each other as equals, as citizens of a moment in which time and place may be reframed.

In *Abide*, music provides an arena for relation. In the blues, relation is graphed through borrowings and quotative talk-back; there, elegy and eulogy are notes on the same scale. If the cultural politics of the past few decades may have held that white ears can hear the blues only at a distance, if at all, relation may allow the blues (or the exchanges that define the blues or musics that descend from the blues, like jazz and hip-hop) to become a space (however disturbed or distorted) in which ownership and ownership's historical specters can be inverted, moved from the root position to a minor third, while the call-and-response happens in the first position.

Within the arena of music, my poetic self and my poetic others—or my ethical self and my ethical others—approach one another, and this approach becomes the blue note and the *blueshift*. In astronomy it is observed, that when an object approaches the viewer, the light cast by that object shifts to the blue end of the spectrum; the blue light arrives first. If we are approaching one another, the light of our approach is the blue light, the light and tone of the blues.

# Acknowledgments

Thanks, first, to the editors and readers of the following journals in which some of these poems appeared (or are soon to appear), sometimes in slightly different forms:

*Greensboro Review*—"Mayflower" and "Exploded View"
*Kenyon Review*—"Cry of the Occasion"
*The Laurel Review*—"Tape Loop" and "Abide (crepuscule)"
*Literary Imagination*—"Letter Hidden in a Letter to Cy Twombly"
    and "Letter Written in the Dark"
*Memorious*—"Abide," "Feedback Loop," "Laws of Conservation,"
    "Letter Written on a Hundred Dollar Bill," and "Postscript to
    Silence"
*Ninth Letter*—"Letter Written in the Breath"
*Pleiades*—"The Voice of Woody Guthrie Wakes in an Antenna in
    Okemah, Oklahoma," "Letter from Okemah," and "Letter to
    Be Read by Furnace Light"
*Ploughshares*—"Letter Written in Black Water and Pearl"
*Prime Number*—"*te lyra pulsa manu* or something like that"
*The Rumpus*—"Letter to Be Wrapped around a 12-Inch Disc"
*Southern Quarterly*—"Letter Written in Someone Else's Hand"
*The Southern Review*—"Letter Written on a Record Sleeve," "Post-
    script Written on a J-Card," "Inscription for Air" and "Postscript"
*Subtropics*—"Epistrophy" and "Dear Brother,"

"Letter Already Broadcast into Space" was the Academy of American Poets' Poem of the Day on November 30, 2011, and is archived on their website.

"*te lyra pulsa manu* or something like that" was composed for and displayed as a part of *Stars Are Symbols*, an exhibition of poetry responding to the work of scientists, curated by Aaron Plasek for the

Other Side Arts in Denver, Colorado, in April 2009. The poem responded to the work on the binary star Beta Lyrae by the University of Denver's Jamie Lomax.

My gratitude to the University of Colorado Denver for leave time that allowed me to complete this book with time, space, and support from Kenyon College and Emory University's James Weldon Johnson Institute for the Study of Race and Difference.

Personal thanks to my friends and fellows who read these poems, individually and sometimes together, who were my audience, and who gathered more: Dan Albergotti, Hadara Bar-Nadav, Brian Barker, Nicky Beer ("The Dude abides"), Stacey Lynn Brown, Peter Campion, Jennifer Clarvoe, Martha Collins, Julie Delliquanti, John T. Edge, Thomas Sayers Ellis, Tarfia Faizullah, Jennifer Faust, Beth Ann Fennelly, Morgan Frank, John Gallaher, Natalie Giarratano, Susan Glisson, Garrett Hongo, Ailish Hopper, Jennifer Horne, Randall Horton, Andrew Hudgins, Major Jackson, Rodney Jones, David Keplinger, Hank Klibanoff, Jeanne Lieby, David Lynn, Beth Marzoni, Adrian Matejka, Nick McRae, Tyler Meier, Wayne Miller, Joshua Poteat, Dave Smith, Eric Smith, Brian Spears, Tess Taylor, Jeanie Thompson, Natasha Trethewey, Jon Tribble, Allen Tullos, Wendy S. Walters, David Wojahn, Joe York, and Kevin Young.

And thanks to my family, for all the stories and histories, and especially Sarah for helping me put time back in order.

## Other Books in the Crab Orchard Series in Poetry